P9-BYS-038

SERVE2WIN

SERVE2WIN

EIGHT STEPS TO
MAKING A LIVING & A LIFE

MITCH DURFEE

Copyright © 2017 by Mitch Durfree

First Edition

All rights reserved. No part of this book may be reproduced in any form or by any electronic or mechanical means including information storage and retrieval systems without permission in writing from the author. The only exception is by a reviewer, who may quote short excerpts in a review.

Although the author and publisher have made every effort to ensure that the information in this book was correct at press time, the author and publisher do not assume and hereby disclaim any liability to any party for any loss, damage, or disruption caused by errors or omissions, whether such errors or omissions result from negligence, accident, or any other cause. The advice and contents in this book are the author's opinion. The author is not making any claims or promises.

Printed in the United States of America

ISBN Paperback: 978-1-947368-07-1
ISBN eBook: 978-1-947368-08-8
LCN: 2017945897

Interior Design: Ghislain Viau

To all those willing to be vulnerable and risk failure
to put the interests of others before their own.

CONTENTS

ACKNOWLEDGEMENTS

EVERYONE HAS A BOOK INSIDE THEM, AND WITHOUT each and every one of you, this book wouldn't have been possible!

To my mom and dad, I will never truly be able to express my sincere appreciation!

To my grandparents who taught me how to be so generous.

To my incredible brothers in arms who I can call on and ask for anything—big, small, or crazy. You are always there for me!

To Ben, Jordon, and Jonathan. You three have always had my back. The tiny adventures we would get ourselves in will always be my proudest moments.

To my family: Michelle, there is nothing like the smile of our beautiful daughter, Brooklyn. Thank you for the endless encouragement, support, and for keeping my spirits up and giving me all the reasons to never give up!

To Jay, Jeff, Lucas, Joe, and to the rest of my Wolfpack. You operate at such a high level every day. The connections, contributions, and collaborations are never-ending. You keep me on my toes, hold me accountable, and remind me to do the things I often forget to do, pushing all of us to new levels of greatness!

But most of all, to the Garcia family. You have always been a rock for me! Juan taught me so much and showed me exactly what it meant to give more to others than you could possibly dream of giving.

FOREWORD

WHEN I FIRST BECAME AWARE OF THE HIGH-powered phenomenon that is Mitch Durfee, it was through all the local channels he was so effectively using in order to market his first business, Grunts Move Junk. To say the least, I was impressed.

Let me hasten to add that I am not easily impressed by marketing campaigns. Having owned a graphic design company for over two decades, I know good art, effective design, and professional marketing when I see them combined in a campaign. So I simply couldn't get over the fact that Mitch's marketing didn't come from a national advertising/marketing firm. In fact, I was so impressed by his talent that I reached out to him and arranged a meeting.

As you might expect, we talked about digital marketing—where the most interesting marketing is occurring these days.

1

And the difference between Mitch's approach and my own could not have been more clear: He was running on high-octane fuel, zipping around at the speed of light, while I was slowly and methodically covering similar ground. (Much later, I learned that Mitch listens to audiobooks while playing them three times faster than normal, something he calls "the four-minute mile" effect. I tried this once. And let's just say it wasn't for me.)

Over the next two years, Mitch and I collaborated on several projects, both marketing campaigns and speaking engagements for business seminars. We also teamed up for Mitch's ongoing personal growth efforts, attending motivational workshops by nationally known experts together. Then, we had the idea of creating a Mastermind group. We drew nearly two dozen local people whose goals were a fit with those Mitch and I had in mind for our respective futures.

Because of my long exposure to Mitch the marketer, Mitch the businessperson, and Mitch the high-speed guy who's both inspiration and friend, I can't recommend this new book by him highly enough. And if you, like many of us, have a passion for doing something big or unusual with your life—feeling, perhaps, that you want to transcend the mundane, middle-of-the-road life so many of us settle for—get a copy of *Serve 2 Win*.

It's a book that will speak to you, fanning the flames of your inner excitement, and pushing you to the next level. Once you read it, get ready for a life of the kind of fulfillment you may have dreamed about—but were afraid wasn't within your ability to achieve. That's because Mitch is a great teacher, a great role model, a great friend to have on your journey toward success as an entrepreneur. And most especially, if you feel guided by a wish to serve others.

—Jay Cummings

THERE HAS TO BE MORE TO LIFE

YEARS BEFORE I BECAME A SUCCESSFUL ENTREPRE-neur who owns three businesses, I left the military and returned to the States, where I used one of my marketable skills—repairing and rebuilding car engines—to earn a living for the better part of a year. It was during this time that I had a number of realizations, one of which I still remember quite vividly:

It had been another long and exhausting day. I felt like I was having a "gut" attack. My stomach was in knots from tiredness and anxiety, because everything in my life was piling up and weighing on me, more heavily by the day.

Every time I worked extra hours and took on more responsibility, it never went anywhere. I didn't get a promotion. All I got was more work, my boss having realized that he could use me to do work after hours that others refused to do.

I kept saying to myself, "There has to more to life than this!"

It was soon after I'd repeated this mantra for the umpteenth time that I realized that it was up to me to make changes in my life. No one was going to help me get anywhere but me.

Fortunately, you're not in that same boat. I can help you get to where you want to go, as a self-employed entrepreneur, because—with a little help from a handful of business and motivational experts—I figured out the best and quickest way to get there myself.

As you read about the eight steps I recommend in the upcoming chapters, remember I've been where you are now. And so, if you'll follow me, we'll get you where you really want to be in life—doing it sooner and better, together.

CHAPTER 1

WHAT DO YOU WANT TO DO WITH YOUR LIFE?

REMEMBER WHEN YOU WERE SEVEN AND YOUR grandmother (or uncle or aunt) smiled down at you kindly to ask, "So young man (young woman), what do you want to be when you grow up?"

Invariably, your answer reflected whatever you'd seen on television, or online, or happened to read in a book.

"A firefighter," you declared, stoutly. "A Grammy Award–winning singer," you chirped, with a little lilt in your voice. And, if you were *that* sort of kid, you might have answered, "President of the United States."

But when you grew up, just a few years later, the world looked very different than it did when you had to tilt your head back to see an adult looking down at you, expectantly. The question had changed, too.

The Importance of Purpose

Instead of asking what role you wanted to play, the relevant question had become: What do you want to accomplish—what purpose do you find meaningful enough to dedicate your life to?

For many of us, the answer to what we want to do is lost beneath the ever-changing demands of daily life. All of which seem to hide our deeply meaningful and gratifying purpose under a thousand and one mundane details.

Still, it's a good idea to ask ourselves that question; the answer can illuminate what's buried deep within us—which may, in turn, reveal a path forward that we might otherwise miss.

So what do you want to do with your life? And if you're not at all sure, how do you find out?

For me, the answer was always closely aligned with a tradition in my family; in fact, I got a leg up in this regard, having almost always known I would follow my grandfather, father, uncle, and older sister into military service. I grew up wanting to serve my country; it came with my DNA. But I know that's not true for everyone.

Very few grow up the way I did, with pre-existing answers. Just as few of us know what direction our lives will take when we're very young—which is, I think, how it should be. We need to know what life is like, from an adult perspective, before we'll know what we can contribute, and also where we can make the most wholehearted contribution.

Okay, so now that you're no longer a child, and have several years—maybe quite a few years—of life experience to guide you, what do you want to do with your life?

What's Easy for You, Hard for Others?

To bring your life experience into sharper focus, ask yourself what you're good at, what you can do with relatively little effort, although it may be difficult for others to do.

Know what that is? Good. And if not, let's get to it from another angle: What makes you feel happy and energized? It could be anything—from the obvious (a day at the beach, working out at the gym, wandering through an antique barn), to the oddball (my obsession with studying real estate catalogs in my early twenties, for example, or a high school friend's goal of visiting every state park before age thirty).

Betting on Yourself

Now, let's take what makes you happy, and place it in the context of this idea: What if you could combine whatever energizes you with the experience of running your own business—wouldn't *that* be worth aspiring to?

Being your own boss is a really enticing dream, one that just about every employed person has had. Especially while stuck in traffic during Monday morning rush hours.

Me, too. I had that dream, myself, and I figured out how to make it my reality before I turned thirty. Once I became my own boss, though, I discovered something lurking below the surface, which was this: What made being in charge *truly* energizing was my much-expanded ability to help others.

You'll see where I'm headed, once I recap: When I'd figured out how to do what I do best, *and* own my own business doing it, *and* established my company's culture on a foundation of service—baked into it from day one—I felt like I'd scored a trifecta: my own three-way win.

Why I Wrote This Book

I wrote this book with the idea of showing *you* how to accomplish something similar: your own trifecta of doing what you're good at, doing it as your own boss, and helping others while you do.

But before we get started on helping you achieve your three-way win, I'd like to pause here and ask whether you've experienced, as I have, this wonderful, unanticipated result: Have you felt "organically" happy after helping someone— whether it's helping them with something big or something small?

If so, could that mean that you, too, have the service gene humming along inside your personal GPS? Let me just say that I'm not at all surprised. Many of us can't help but feel an unexpected happiness bubbling up whenever we assist another person. Not only does it give a little lift to our day, it makes our whole existence feel especially worthwhile.

Serving Isn't Servitude

For some of us, though, the prospect of basing one's life and new business on service to others comes uncomfortably close to the unpleasant feeling of being used. In other words, being a kind of human doormat—being stepped on while others benefit.

However, I'd like to point out that there is a clear and *critical* difference between wanting to help others who genuinely need and want your help, and being obligated, whether by cultural expectations or circumstances, to lend a hand. To illustrate that difference, here's something that happened to me on a wintry day in Vermont, where I've lived, for the most part, my whole life.

If you know anything about New England, you know that snow visits regularly and leaves behind several feet of the white, landscape-altering stuff overnight. On one such occasion, I was out early, working my part-time snow-plowing job, when I happened to see a woman about half a block away shoveling her car out of her driveway, presumably to get to work. I thought to myself, "Once I'm done here, I'll go down and see if she needs a hand."

Ten minutes later, I pulled into the road and drove toward her, only to hear her call out, "I can't believe you're not going to help me!"

Immediately, I felt conflicted. This was not how I imagined things would go; not at all. In a split second, though, I decided that helping someone who treated me like a servant *obligated* to remove her snow was not part of my job description. I could have patiently explained that I was going to help, but her verbal attack soured my good intentions.

Instead, I allowed myself to get bitten by the underlying hostility in her remark, and called back, "Have a nice day!"

It wasn't a nice thing to say, because I so obviously didn't mean it. But it was the least offensive thing I could think of at the time.

Of course, in retrospect, I questioned both our behaviors. Should I have salvaged the situation by patiently explaining how her remark had the effect of driving me away, rather than making me want to help?

Could she have offered me hot coffee on a cold winter morning, a gesture guaranteed to make me feel like I was another human being to her, which would, in turn, make me want to respond in kind?

Perhaps next time we'll both find a better way.

The moral of this story is that serving others does not mean engaging in servitude. It means reaching out to others, when the opportunity arises, with a feeling of wanting to help—because you and they are fellow human beings, people engaged in contributing to the well-being of the human family, which is worldwide, as I'll explain later on.

In other words, you help because you see other people as friends, and even distant relatives—which is actually the case. In 1987, geneticists discovered that every human being alive on the Earth at the present time is descended from "Mitochondrial Eve," a common female ancestor who lived in Africa 200,000 years ago.

So that snowy-day woman and I are probably cousins twenty or thirty times removed, and we could have tried a little harder to recognize our status as relatives within our common humanity.

Your Life Plan Trifecta

Getting back to the purpose of this book—which is to help you win your life plan trifecta, by finding out what you're uniquely good at doing, figuring out how to start your own business doing it, and finding ways to help others while you do—from my own experience with the above enterprise, I know that certain methods and tools can be incredibly beneficial in achieving that triple win.

For instance, nothing works better (and harder) than having a positive mental attitude (PMA) about what you want to accomplish. Nothing. I know this because I've seen how its opposite can wreak havoc on the best plans made by good people with remarkable talent.

It's just not helpful to have a terrific plan—one truly appropriate for who you are, and what you're good at—but keep beating yourself up with negative thoughts ("I could never do this. . . . I'm not the type who gets these kinds of breaks from other people. . . . It just won't work.").

Here's what you can do, instead: Go ahead and fake an attitude of believing in yourself, and if you do that long enough, you may find, after a while, that you actually do believe it. The results that emerge will be astonishing, because PMA is like Miracle-Gro for your life.

In addition to having a PMA, I've found that it's best to approach any life plan from a SMART perspective—that is, by setting goals for yourself that are, as motivational speaker and author Tony Robbins and many others have said, **S**pecific, **M**easurable, **A**ttainable, **R**ealistic, and **T**imely.

The only problem I've found with this acronym is that what seems attainable and realistic, right now, may not be big enough to encompass your long-range, meaningful-purpose goal.

So cheat a little, in a good way; add some imagination to what's attainable and realistic until you get there. For instance, you might have a goal of being a well-known public speaker on a topic you know a lot of about. But let's say you're not too keen on speaking in public, just now.

Here's what you can do: Keep your big goal, but break it down into smaller goals that are attainable and realistic right now. You could hire a speaking coach, or join Toastmasters, or just practice by yourself in front of your dog for a week or two, until you feel ready to go on to the next-level realistic goal that is sitting on the path to your larger overall goal.

I'll talk more about SMART goals later on, but for now, it's enough to know that they're a good tool for developing the pragmatic muscles you'll need to arrive at your personal trifecta.

Finally, I want to mention a core tool that has always helped me move higher, faster, and arrive at my overall goals according to the schedule I've devised, and that's having a network, a mastermind group to bounce ideas around with, to get and give information to, and to be held accountable for everything I say I'm going to do, when I'm going to do it.

My group is like my goal-achievement family, my buddies in success. There's nothing more motivating, helpful, and kick-ass than having a bunch of friends who meet regularly to help each other work on ambitious goals, and who share that journey with you, every step of the way.

So there you have it: the purpose behind this book, what you can expect from reading it, and one more thing.

My commitment to you is that I'll always be available to answer your questions through my website (Serve2Win.com). And so, as you work your way through this book, if you want to know a little more about the way something works, just send me an email.

We're in this together, me and you.

CHAPTER 2

MY JOURNEY

FROM BEING *IN* THE SERVICE
... TO BEING *OF* SERVICE

I COME FROM A VERMONT FAMILY, THREE GENERA-tions of whom have served in various branches of the military. And as I mentioned in the previous chapter, it was this familial tradition that shaped my career aspirations from a very early age.

What I *didn't* mention was that, also from an early age, I was an entrepreneurial go-getter. By age eleven, I was doing odd jobs for money and liked the idea of being in business for myself—perhaps a bit more than I liked mowing lawns and shoveling snow.

The Service Secret

Aside from being a business owner (as I thought of myself, even then), what I secretly liked most was the warm glow that came from helping people who needed my help. More than anything else, the happiness that rose up in me whenever someone expressed gratitude for my work was a feeling that never, ever paled.

Years later, it was one aspect of my decision to enlist in the army at eighteen (I raised my hand to join at seventeen, but had to wait another year, until I graduated from high school). And, several years after that, it was also one of a handful of reasons that contributed to my decision to leave the military. To illustrate why this was the case, I'd like to take a slight detour and recount a few of the life-changing experiences I had during two army deployments.

Gifts That Make a Difference

Along with thousands of other young Americans, I was sent to Iraq to fight our ongoing war, but the other part of our stated military mission was a lot more to my liking, as it involved "winning hearts and minds" through impromptu conversations and the goodwill of giving small gifts.

We often handed out relatively inexpensive presents to children—things that, to our American eyes, didn't seem all that persuasive. Pretty soon, though, we learned that a soccer ball or a backpack could seem miraculous to an Iraqi child. That response touched us, at a time when we were living daily with the fear that we might not make it back from our next mission.

When Giving Is a Cultural Value

There were many other heartwarming experiences that I carried home with me after thirty-six months in the army, but another one—which occurred when I used a few vacation days to scuba dive (my all-time favorite recreational pursuit) in the Philippines—impressed me at an even deeper level.

At the end of another exhilarating day spent diving in clear turquoise water, one of the Filipino guides on our scuba boat, whom I'd become friendly with during my fourteen-day stay, invited me to his house for dinner with his family. What was so astonishing about his invitation was the fact that he had barely enough money to feed his family. And yet, here he was inviting a tourist to share whatever he had. I went, of course, because I enjoy the adventure of meeting people, but I took along bags of vegetables, fruit, and fish from a local market, hoping it would help him out—for a few days, at least.

The reason I'm sharing these experiences is because, while our culture's most widely accepted core values are very connected to personal survival and bootstrap individualism, the core value in the Philippines is to ensure the happiness (survival) of others—even relative strangers—by being as giving as possible. I think they have the right idea.

Helping Others Helps You, Too

In my experience, the best way to ensure my own survival was to ensure the survival of those around me. I relearned that concept in the army, of course, when I depended on the guys in my unit during dangerous missions, and because (in addition to the military values of loyalty, duty, honor, integrity, personal courage) we were indoctrinated with the central value of selfless service—since selflessness is certainly one aspect of living in potentially fatal conditions.

Apart from the army, though, I'd pretty much figured this out as a child in New England, when shoveling out my neighbors' cars, so they could get to work, helped me launch my kid-size business. I also had my grandfather to thank for a leg up in this area; now a retired teacher, he likes doing things for others in ways that couldn't reveal him to be those good deeds' source. When I asked him why he did all these things anonymously—when I was older and knew enough to be amazed—his answer was that it made him feel good; helping out increased his sense of enjoying life, gave him new energy, and made him feel his best. That's good enough for me. As Tony Robbins once said, "The secret to living is giving."

Not Meant to Be

My time in the military wasn't always heartwarming, but not for the reason you might think. When I enlisted, I envisioned a twenty-year career for myself, largely in the Special Forces. But I wasn't able to do either. Each time I tried to put myself in a good position to enter the elite Special Forces unit, I was thwarted. And so, after repeated tries, I decided that it was time to get out of the military and return to the States, in order to explore other opportunities.

Once I was home, though, I felt as if I'd fallen behind my peers who had attended college while I was serving overseas. To me, they seemed to have a better basis for beginning their lives as adults, while I had bet on making the army my career and lost that bet—it hadn't panned out the way I thought it would.

Meanwhile, I needed to make a civilian living, and so, after spending months repairing an old Jeep (I worked on that car as if my life depended on it), I decided to launch a car mechanic business with a like-minded friend who was good with engines. This worked out really well—so well, in fact, that we ended up signing an overseas contract to fix military vehicles, when they got blown up during the war in Afghanistan.

Fast forward about fifteen months, and I'd realized that I couldn't do this forever; each and every twelve-hour day, seven days of the week, was virtually the same. And there was no possibility of progress, no career path. But apart from the wearying sameness, the other reason I woke up was because I'd been listening to inspirational audio books, like *The Seven Habits of Highly Effective People* by Stephen Covey, and the classic *Think and Grow Rich* by Napoleon Hill.

Back to Square One

The influence of those books was transformative, in hindsight, because they gave me something new to aspire to, along with a rudimentary road map for how to attain any aspiration I might have. When I got back home, though, I felt lost all over again. There was no support system, and no one to talk to about what I'd been through, since my experience in the military, followed by returning overseas to restore damaged vehicles, was not shared by anyone. That's how it seemed at the time, anyway, and I struggled to fit into the life of my small town.

Eventually, I had an idea for a business that was, as they say, "staring me in the face": I decided to launch a moving business that employed veterans, firefighters, emergency medical technicians (EMTs), and first responders—people, in other words, who'd worked in situations so stressful they'd been pushed to their outer limits, and needed a little help adjusting to "normal" life. I called my business "Grunts Move Junk." And my semi-unstated mission was to help vets and those who'd been in high-stress, service-to-others jobs get over their anxiety-provoking reentry into regular life, by giving them a job, first. And second, helping them discover what they really wanted to do, and how to get the training to do it. In short, Grunts Move Junk offered them everything I myself needed when I returned, but had a hard time finding.

As I'll reveal in upcoming chapters, I didn't stop there, but eventually launched several more businesses, as the need—and the desire—for them became clear. But Grunts Move Junk was my first business, the one that has allowed me to transition successfully from being *in* the service to being *of* service, to my clients and employees, each and every day.

CHAPTER 3

THE EIGHT STEPS
AN INTRODUCTION

YOU MAY RECALL FROM THE OPENING CHAPTER that there are eight key steps my business coaching clients and I used to become self-employed small business owners. In this chapter, I'll offer an overview of the way that these steps—or tools, as they actually are—can prove beneficial. After that, I'll shine a brighter light on each one in upcoming chapters, while also clarifying how they can help you reach your business goal.

Before we begin, though, here they are again, so you'll know where we're headed:

1. **Having the Right Values**
2. **Deciding What Your (True) Goals Are**

3. Building Your Peer-Support Network
4. Having a Positive Mental Attitude (PMA)
5. Taking Action
6. Protecting Your Time
7. Building Your Working Team
8. Positioning Yourself to Win

What Does It Mean to Have the "Right Values"?

As you can probably guess, I'm using *values* as a kind of shorthand for the essential message of this book, which is: If you base your business (and your life) on using your skills and talents to serve others, you'll "win" in ways that are gratifying in a pragmatic way, and that prove to be truly miraculous in other ways, as well.

That's because when you are primarily interested in serving others, you are putting your new business in the best possible position to establish itself, to grow well, and to thrive, over time.

Why, you may wonder, is that true, and how does it work?

It works for several reasons—reasons that are, again, both practical and nothing short of miraculous. On the practical side, people are drawn to businesses that have about them a feeling of being engaged in serving their clients and customers. It's a feeling that can't be faked, so people respond to the sincerity behind it. The miraculous part comes into play because, when customers or clients have good—and sometimes heartwarming—experiences with a business, they will tell others. And your business' reputation will ripple out far and wide, into the world. Once you reach the "peak reputation point," all that good feeling will start to come back to you in the form of new business, repeat business, other offers, helpful assistance, and a whole lot more.

Not only will you find that when you act in ways that send out a positive and helpful message it comes back to you many times over, this is also the best magnet for generating the conditions that will allow your business to thrive.

Here's a quick way to remember this: "Serve 2 Win," the title of this book, is no empty catchphrase. It is, instead, the key to winning in business—and in life.

How Do You Find & Embrace Your Core Goals?

Your next step will require a bit of introspection. Briefly, a core goal is one that's big enough for you to grow into, and yet so completely aligned with who you are (your interests, your energies, whatever's uniquely you) that it makes complete sense for you to pursue it.

If such a goal doesn't come to mind in, say, thirty seconds or so, then write down everything you find exciting and interesting, things that have been your passionate pursuits, for—if not most of your life—then for a handful of years. Most likely, you'll see one or two interests that really speak to you, interests that could become your best choice for an entrepreneurial business.

Once you have a good candidate for your core goal, check in with yourself about whether or not it inspires you to act. Do you feel energized if you imagine owning a business that offers, let's say, dog grooming, landscaping, artisanal bread, or something else entirely?

If so, then move to the next phase, which is to *make a commitment* to your business goal by writing it down; sharing it with friends (so they'll keep you accountable, by regularly asking about your progress toward small, incremental goals); and listing all the smaller steps you need to take in order to reach your larger goal.

Building Your Peer-Support Network

It may not be obvious, when you envision yourself as a self-starting, independent entrepreneur, but having a peer-support network is one of the best strategies for getting where you want to go.

Among other things, a network of peers engaged in pursuing challenging, long-term goals (the way you are), can keep you on track, week after week, month after month, like nothing else can.

But you want to choose your peer network wisely, and I'll talk about this in greater detail in Chapter Six. Briefly, though, aim to assemble a group of people who are doing great things, whose sense of what they can accomplish is large and uplifting. To reach your goal, you need to surround yourself with peers who are growing and stretching in their lives, who want to achieve something unique to them, just as you do.

Got PMA?

Here's something so life-altering, and yet, so within your control, that you can hardly believe it would make any difference in what shows up in your life. And what is it? It's your frame of mind, your mental mind-set, your attitude, that influences how you feel and how you react to everything that happens, from one hour of the day to the next. And if you know how to instantly create a Positive Mental Attitude (PMA), you'll put yourself way ahead of your competition from the get-go.

Here's what you need to do: Recognize that your energy level is directly related to your attitude, which is in turn produced by your perceptions about what is happening in your life. Also recognize that your perceptions can alter in mere seconds, and along with them, both your attitude and your energy level.

Here's an example: Let's say that one of your clients has promised to send along a deposit for a high-end service, so you can get started on delivering the first phase, but on Monday, there's no sign of an electronic payment, and you feel discouraged to the point of making it into a mental catastrophe—meaning you start to have all kinds of self-doubts and wonder if this client is perhaps a little less than honest, too.

Ten minutes later, you get a call from your client who says that, since he was going to be in your neighborhood, he decided to drop off a check, instead, so he could talk with you about not just the service he already wants, but a couple others he saw on your website over the weekend. In no more than five seconds, you jump out of despair into total confidence and happiness. You're on top of the world!

What happened? That good news shifted your whole attitude from negative to positive in less time than it takes to snap your fingers three times. And that's the magic of attitude. You can control it—as easily as you control your thoughts, which will, in turn, transform how you feel.

The Importance of Taking Action

So there you are, all set up with your service mind-set, your perfect business as your long-term goal, your peer support group, your PMA, and . . . So what's next?

Of course, taking action toward your goal is next. Without action, the best plans, approach, and attitude will get you exactly nowhere, and that's not where you want to be.

So, here's the thing: to take action, you need a road map. You need a list of all the things you need to do, in the order of their priority. For instance, when I got back from overseas, I was talking to my friend and informal mentor, Robert Bloch, who directs the BYOBiz program at Champlain College, telling him what I wanted to do—how I wanted to start my own business—and he encouraged me to write down all the steps I needed to take. That's exactly what I needed to hear. The weekend after our conversation, I washed my car, filled its tank, and drove six hours to buy a truck. When I got home, I built a website, and then I created flyers to advertise my company's services locally.

In my case, the business worked. It took off, and three years later, it's still going strong. But that doesn't always happen. Sometimes, you start a business and it's a learning experience, so when you start your next business, you already have a good idea of the things you need to do, what will work, and what will not. It's a learning curve, and in my experience, it never stops "curving," as there are always new things to learn, new challenges to surmount. But that's what makes it so much fun; there is never a dull interlude when you own your own business. You are always stretching toward new goals.

Time Is Far More Valuable Than Money

As an entrepreneur / small business owner, your time is really your most precious resource. We all have the same number of hours in a day, week, and month, but how we use those hours can be smart, effective, and productive—or the opposite. We can fail to see how valuable our time really is, and instead waste it on activities that get us no closer to our main goal; it's up to us which of these two ways we want to use our time.

Meanwhile, here's a useful tool for corralling your time resource, so it yields results rather than regrets: Give yourself a definite time frame to accomplish each of your prioritized tasks. The reason being, if you tell yourself you have a month to do something, you'll probably start working on it two days before that month is up and may not have enough time to complete it—which will create havoc with other parts of your business and all your other tasks.

Far better to tell yourself that you have the next three days to get your task done, and that's all the time you get; after that, you've got a list of other tasks you have to devote your time to, and so you have no choice but to get this done in that time frame. As an added incentive, tell someone in your peer support group that if you don't get this task done in three days, you'll pay him or her a hundred dollars. Write out the check and hand it over, with the stipulation that your peer-group member can deposit it if you don't get your task completed by a specific day, at a specific time. You'll be amazed at how motivating this strategy is—how easily it revs up your sense of urgency and your ability to be efficient with your available time.

Here's another strategy that can help you cut to the chase when you're faced with a mountain of tasks that all look as though they need to be done at the same time. Recognize that there are four ways to divide up these "do" list tasks: Do them. Delegate them. Delay them. Or decide they aren't worth doing. When you divide all your jobs into those four categories, you always know that you need to first delegate the delegate-able jobs; and second, you need to prioritize the ones you are going to do; and third, you need to schedule a time to do the jobs you're delaying right now; and fourth, you need to discard the jobs that you've decided not to do. This is simple, efficient, and very effective; in other words, the kind of thing that small business owners like best.

Have Business Team, Will Succeed

Once your business enters its second phase and is successful enough that you, the owner, can afford to no longer do every single task your business requires, it's time to hire people to take over parts of your workload, or perhaps outsource them to a business specializing in that task (bookkeeping, for example).

In my experience, the most critical aspect of this shift from the phase in which you, the owner, do everything, to the phase in which you begin hiring staff or outsourcing some business tasks, is the "A," "B," and "C" players concept, and their crucial differences. Let me explain.

An "A" player will take initiative, once you give him or her a position in your company, and will "own" the job in the sense of taking responsibility not only for it, but for everything that contributes to it. So let's say you, the business owner, ask your "A" player to mail some bills while she's out picking up office supplies. Not only will she do the things you asked her to do, she'll pick up more stamps while she's at the post office, because she knows the business is nearly out of them, and she'll buy copies of local papers because she knows it's a good idea for you to advertise your business locally, but you'll need to know the requirements for each paper. While she's out, she'll also gas up the company van because she knows you have to deliver boxes of your product tomorrow to a location that's about seventy-five miles away.

If, on the other hand, you ask your "B" player to accomplish the same tasks, he may indeed mail the bills and pick up the office supplies, but he'll not think ahead and won't take any responsibility beyond the specific tasks he's been asked to do. The "C" player, on the other hand, may pick up the office supplies but leave the bills on the dashboard when he stops for lunch, and then he'll return to the office after two hours, or about an hour and a half beyond what both jobs required, and he's forgotten all about going to the post office.

The moral of this story is: Do not hire "B" or "C" players. They will only waste your time, because they need so much supervision for even minor tasks, and they're a huge drain on you and your company. They will also demoralize your "A" players, who may, in frustration, go to a more "A"-player-filled company.

What Does It Mean to "Position Yourself to Win"?

While the idea of being your own boss is appealing to at least half the people in any given group, the reality that you need to be willing to accomplish more with your time nearly every day, in order to get there, is not so appealing, which may be why fewer people go into business for themselves.

But the truth is, if you want to "win" at creating your own business, you need to start doing things while you're still working for someone else that will move you toward that goal. The bottom line: You'll have to do one and a half, if not two jobs—sometimes for quite a long time, a year or more—in order to position yourself to "win" at owning your own business.

Here's how I did it: When I returned from overseas for the last time, I got a job working for a car repair place as a mechanic, even though my long-term goal was to become a real estate agent and investor. And so, while working on cars, I used headphones to listen to real estate material and study for my real estate licensing exam. Three months later, I passed my exam and quit my job working for someone else.

Whatever your current situation is, you can position yourself to become self-employed, if that's your true goal, by working toward it while you work at something else. It's true that not everyone will want to work that hard. But when you consider the benefits of being self-employed versus the tenuous proposition (layoffs being common) of being employed by someone else, you may find that it's more than worth it to you.

In the next chapter, we'll take a more in-depth look at the concept of "values" as a way to get your new business up and running.

CHAPTER 4

STEP 1

HAVE THE RIGHT VALUES

YOU'VE MOST LIKELY HEARD OF THE "LAW OF Attraction." Widely popularized, this universal law refers to the often-observed phenomenon whereby what you think about frequently, especially when accompanied by strong feelings, will sooner or later show up in your life. It makes no difference if you focus on something positive, or not; when your thoughts and feelings are aligned with the belief that what you envision will manifest, whatever it is will eventually appear.

That being the case, it's in your best interest, as a business owner, to focus on (think about, visualize, and cultivate your belief in) the positive outcomes you wish to see in your business— while, at the same time, avoiding being stuck in worry and anxiety about any number of unwanted outcomes, relative to your business.

How Your Values "Power Up" the Law of Attraction

Apart from its use as a manifesting strategy—one I recommend to all my coaching clients—there's a more direct reason why I included the Law of Attraction in a chapter on aligning with values that have the ability to inspire. It's because your essential values provide the emotional power you need when using the Law of Attraction to succeed at launching and building your business.

Here's another way to look at it: What you focus on manifesting will primarily be imbued with your desire to serve others, *or* it will be imbued with something else—perhaps money, success, and power. It's true that most business owners want to earn money and be successful while having the power to direct their business and personal lives. But when their only aim is to produce those three results, something far more important is missing, which is this: how their business will contribute to the greater good.

Basing your company on serving others—having a desire to improve the lives of your clients and customers—will make a huge difference in the success of your enterprise. That's because your interest in serving people will ripple outward far and wide before it comes back to you—bringing with it people, circumstances, and outcomes that mirror what you sent out into the world, and often in magnified form.

I have seen this happen in my coaching clients' businesses, and in my own companies, too. It can even happen with your employees. Here's an example from my first business, Grunts Move Junk.

Because I grew up in a small Vermont town—the same town where I live now—I know most of the young men who resettled here after serving in the military. One of them is an acquaintance I knew in high school—whom I'll call Tom Johnson, to protect his privacy—and who was always cheerful and smiling, a helpful, friendly guy who got married and started a family soon after he returned. A couple years later, Tom lost his job (through no fault of his own) in the same week that his house burned down.

When I heard what happened, I reached out and offered him a job at Grunts Move Junk, and Tom started working for us the next day, thanking me for the opportunity. I was amazed—though I shouldn't have been—that, in less than six months, Tom had become our star recruiter, bringing in no less than eight new accounts during those months. He attracted them with his pleasing personality, despite the fact that he'd just suffered a huge personal loss and, needless to say, he more than repaid the business.

Waking-Up Thoughts:
Setting the Intention to Succeed

Basing your business on serving others isn't simply a way of benefiting *them*—and by extension, the world—it's a way to benefit yourself at the same time. For instance, if you spend your first waking moments each morning, as I do, telling yourself that you are going to serve as many people as possible, it has an uplifting effect on your energy. You feel happy, cheerful, and motivated.

But if you instead tell yourself how you'd better figure out how to attract a handful of lucrative clients, it feels as if you are mentally and emotionally setting yourself up to fight for what you want from an uncooperative world, which seems like an unpleasant chore. And as a way to start a new day, it's certainly not inspiring and uplifting.

Here's what I like to recommend to new business owners or would-be business owners. Recognize that your first waking moments, before you're even out of bed, can be potent with possibility, since you're still in touch with your subconscious mind (the part that drives all we do) before the conscious, waking mind takes over. Take advantage of this very brief time frame to tell yourself good things, to set your intention at a high level, rather than just mentally reviewing that day's to-do list (it can come later).

For instance, you might want to tell yourself that today's goal is to help at least three people, in ways big and small. At the same time, you could tell yourself that you are truly capable of doing great things—or some other message that will give you a feeling of revved-up confidence. There is no point in putting yourself down; it only makes it harder, if not impossible, to do well and to do good things for others. Even if it feels a bit strange, at first, keep telling yourself what a wonderful, courageous, awesome person you are, anyway. Over time, that message will sink into your subconscious mind. And then you'll start to reap the rewards of having enhanced self-acceptance, to the point of even being able to feel more self-love.

One thing to keep in mind about this daily morning ritual is that the most unpleasant people you will ever meet are most likely those who don't like themselves very much. They may not be consciously aware of not liking themselves, but that is often the root cause of bad behavior.

On the other hand, when people like themselves, when they feel good about the person they are—the person they are in the world—they almost *can't* behave badly toward others. Being good to other people begins with being good to yourself; it's one more way that the Law of Attraction works: You attract circumstances into your life that mirror how you feel about yourself—whether you are self-accepting and kind to yourself, or you are not. (If you find that you are not, work on that first—on cultivating the ability to be your own best advocate and "business" partner.)

After Setting Your Intention: Visualize & Affirm Your Goal

Every morning, even before I get out of bed, in addition to telling myself that I'm going to help at least three people today, I tell myself I'm awesome and unstoppable, while adding various expletives for the oomph that they contribute. Then I take a long look at my current-year goal, which I've made into an image I use as the screensaver on my cell phone. That's the reminder exercise I use to kick-start my main-goal-meeting efforts for that day (one year, my goal was to buy a million dollars worth of real estate—more on that later; this year, my goal is to write this book).

And when I look at my goal first thing, it prepares me to take action and be mindful of any opportunity I might otherwise overlook or dismiss; it also focuses my barely awake conscious mind—in addition to my fast-receding subconscious mind—to assist me in achieving that year's main objective.

What I'm actually practicing when I look at my goal on my cell phone each morning is "visualization and affirmation." I visualize my goal as I read the words and look at the image, and I affirm it in the act of reading those words. These small, simultaneous acts support the focusing strategy of setting an intention, making it much more likely that I'll succeed in reaching my goal.

So, I'd like to recommend trying these tools yourself—as you begin to incorporate the Law of Attraction manifestation strategy into your business-building toolkit.

A Few More Thoughts on Inspiring & Empowering Values

One of the simplest things anyone can say about being the kind of person who always lends a hand, who always says a kind word, or who always does the generous thing is that "it doesn't cost anything." And that's true. It doesn't.

But it *does* require a certain kind of humility; you can't be a good person as a marketing strategy, or as a way of attracting new business. Very often, the people we help never help us back—although other people do. At times, it seems as if there's an invisible scale, repaying us when we least expect it.

On the other hand, it's okay to do good things for other people, knowing that it makes you feel good and that doing so uplifts your emotional landscape, often for hours. It's also okay to realize that feeling that uplift may actually attract the very circumstances you'd like to most manifest for your business—or it may not, though often enough, it does. Our mood influences what happens to us, and can do so fairly quickly. Just look at how road rage works: Angry drivers instantly attract other angry drivers, while non-angry drivers stay away because not only do their emotions not match, they are repelled. By the same token, friendly people in a good mood tend to attract other friendly people.

Here's my final question: Which result would you prefer?

It's quite literally up to you which one you will eventually manifest.

CHAPTER 5

STEP 2

SET UP YOUR GOALS

IF YOU'VE ATTENDED A HANDFUL OF WORKSHOPS offered by some of the top ten motivational speakers in this country, you've probably heard a facilitator or two ask a smaller, breakout-session group about their goals.

Going around the circle, most people volunteered one or more goals that they hoped to attain at some point, or someday—although not right now.

And if that breakout facilitator wanted to make a specific point, she might have asked how many of those with a long-term goal had gone so far as to write it down. Going around the circle again, about half that number had taken that next step.

Moving closer to proving her point, the facilitator might have asked how many of those with a written-down goal actually looked at it each day. As it turned out, almost no one took that additional step toward achieving a goal.

Finally, the facilitator may have asked how many were carrying their written-down goals around with them, as a talisman to remind them of their overall goal. As you might expect, not one person said yes, they did that.

What's the moral of this little exercise?

It's simply that, in order to actually achieve a goal, you need to make it part of your daily life in an active way, and do so over time. For it does no good to think you might like to, say, own a holistic retreat sometime in the vague future. Unless you take measured, specific steps toward your goal, each and every day, you'll never make that desire into more than an idle dream—which is, of course, another reason to pick your goals carefully, choosing only those you feel truly motivated to work toward, step by step, day after day.

How to Pick the Right Goal

It can't be overstated: Choosing a goal with built-in motivation is the best possible way to move yourself halfway there, putting you that much closer to achieving it. If, on the other hand, you pick something that seems safe, a goal you could probably achieve without too much trouble, it may seem a bit boring to you, and that means it will be difficult to muster the commitment and energy you need to attain it. Why?

Because you don't care that much about it, as it does nothing for your adrenaline, for the part of you that dreams of doing great things. It's basically boring.

Instead, pick a goal that revs you up, one that inspires you to get out of bed every morning with an eagerness to get started on that day's smaller, specific tasks designed to get you incrementally closer to your larger goal.

How to S-t-r-e-t-c-h Your SMART Goals

Here are two more tools to help you decide which goal is the one most likely to inspire you, while empowering your eagerness to attain it: the Stretch Goal folded within the SMART Goal.

Most business-oriented people have heard of both types of goals, the former being a goal that is sufficiently ambitious to require moving out of your current comfort zone—in other words, stretching—to achieve it. And the latter being an acronym for five elements every workable goal needs to be Specific, Measurable, Attainable, Realistic (reality-based), and Time-Framed (or time-based).

In other words, your goal must be well-defined rather than generalized (buy ten acres near the second bend of the Allagash River near Smallville versus acquire some land). Achieving it must have a measurable end point (like, legally owning the land). It must be something you can realistically find a way to do (get a loan, sell existing assets, earn more money with a second job). And it must have a time frame within which you intend to accomplish it (by November 19 of next year versus in a few years or so).

The magic happens when you combine the focusing and strategizing qualities of your SMART goal with the reaching for a higher-level, ambitious outcome of your Stretch goal—in order to find the most energizing, aspirational outcome you can imagine for yourself. One that is, at the same time, completely doable and realistic in every aspect (and that you can easily break down into daily goals, in order to reach your larger goal, over time).

Okay, so this is where we get back to the service aspect of being an entrepreneur and starting your own business. Because one sure way to rev yourself up is to take advantage of the good feelings, the increase in endorphins (I like to call them "happy hormones") that flood you when you do good things for others. And when your Stretch Goal, folded into your SMART framework, is something that will enhance not only your own life but the lives of others, what better motivation is there; how much more exciting could it be?

The Not-So-Secret Ingredient of Accountability

Meanwhile, even the most inspiring and empowering goal can use the outside help provided by a group of people who will hold you accountable to your daily, weekly, and monthly goals, as well as your big-picture goal.

From firsthand experience, I know that my business networking group has been invaluable to me in creating all my companies—simply because wanting to avoid social "failure" (failing to do what I told a big group of people I was going to do) has the power to motivate me to act even when I'm just a bit afraid I won't succeed, or think I'm way too tired to make the effort. Knowing I have to report back to my business buddies is enough to push me over the edge into actions I might not otherwise have pushed myself to take, but am always glad I did.

So remember to use accountability to your advantage and find or create a group who will hold you to the goals, both small and large, that you set for yourself.

When You Hit the Tough Parts

While finding and working on the right big goal for you is important, I don't want you to think that you can avoid the hard work that goes into creating something worthwhile that will benefit you and others. Because sometimes that work can seem too difficult, too challenging to complete.

We all hit walls, and plateaus, and stuck places in the process of moving forward with our goals. The thing is to not let those glitches own us, but to realize they're just another part of the journey, and then, try stepping back to study the situation, to see if there isn't a way around this particular anthill that, when you're much too close to it, isn't apparent.

That's my fallback position number one, which I also recommend to my coaching clients, when I'm faced with a difficult problem or series of events that leave me temporarily stymied.

My fallback position number two is to step even farther back and think about how I will feel once I attain my goal, whether it's my short-term, this-day-only goal, or my big goal. I try to bask in the feeling of achievement I'll feel, and luxuriate in all the rewarding feelings I'll have. And I think about how I'll be able to legitimately congratulate myself on achieving something that, to be honest, I wasn't entirely sure—at least not every step of the way—that I could achieve.

And then I take all those good feelings and thoughts and direct them at the challenge I'm facing right now, and see if it doesn't act like WD-40 to loosen the stuck parts a little and get me moving forward again.

CHAPTER 6

STEP 3
BUILD YOUR NETWORK

WHEN I FLEW BACK TO THE STATES AFTER SERVING in Afghanistan, I felt the way many returning vets feel: a bit lost and disoriented. But when that initial feeling finally dissipated, I became aware of the need to transition out of military survival mode and enter an ordinary civilian mindset. In the end, it took quite a few months for me to settle in and actually get there.

The next aspect of readapting to life in my small Vermont town was the realization that I only knew a dozen or so people. All my former friends had either moved away or moved on with their lives. So my second struggle was with finding a way to make new friends who could relate to who I was now. What I needed was a way to connect with people interested in the things I was interested in—the strategies, tools, and best practices for becoming a creative entrepreneur and successful small business owner.

The Powerful Support of a Networking Group

Fortunately, I ran into Jay Cummings, a local entrepreneur-turned-marketing executive who shared my interests. We spent hours on Jay's boat talking about marketing, which is an obsession of mine, because it affects almost everything you'd want to do in business. And besides, it's just fascinating.

As our friendship developed, we decided to launch an entrepreneur networking group and soon gathered nearly twenty people by word of mouth. Initially, we were thinking of holding meetings once a month; then a few people argued for a more immersive experience, and we ultimately agreed to meet on a weekly basis. I'm so glad we did.

Our "G19" group has been the single most important element in my continuing success as a business owner. That's been the case for nearly all our members, too, since those weekly, often three-hour networking meetings have resulted in a new confidence, an enhanced ability to take courageous action, and the ultimate achievement of many stretch goals among our members.

For me, personally, our group—which has included professionals in banking, marketing, finance, insurance, real estate, security, fitness, and sales—was instrumental in helping me weather the many ups and downs of launching my three businesses, building and maintaining them, and taking steps to expand into other parts of the country through franchising.

Every step of the way, our networking group has acted like a board of directors for each member's enterprise. Whenever one of us faced a seemingly insurmountable business problem, everyone helped him or her overcome it. Often, we did this by sharing what had worked for us, and what might work in this instance with this member's challenge, as well. Other times, we were able to shorten the journey to success by pooling information to help our members avoid the potential dead ends or wrong turns they were poised to take.

Meanwhile, we've been able to assist each other with challenges that are, you could say, closer to home than a business. Several of our members have been successful in setting a major weight loss goal and reaching it over the course of a year. That's an important achievement because, unless you feel good physically and are healthy, it's difficult to put in a lot of hours working on your business. Our group helped these members by holding them accountable—by caring how well they were doing in meeting their stated goals, week after week.

There is nothing like a group of supportive colleagues to ramp up your motivation and give you the sheer oomph and determination to succeed.

Buying a Million Dollars' Worth of Real Estate

I'd been fascinated by real estate years before I enlisted in the army, but during my deployments, rather than read the magazines other guys were escaping into, I studied real estate catalogs every chance I got. My goal was to replicate the strategy used by all the financially successful people I'd heard of, which was to own a sufficient number of properties to clear six figures each year in passive rental income.

This seemed to me the best way to escape that never-ending work treadmill of trading hours for dollars, in jobs that would never lead anywhere. I didn't want that kind of life for myself. So I took one step after another to put myself on a different track altogether.

My networking group was a continual source of support during the year my goal was to buy real estate properties valued in the aggregate at one million dollars. In part, as I knew I'd have to report back to them each week, and failure was not an option, I immediately started calculating backwards from the end of the year to figure out where I needed to be each month, what I had to accomplish in terms of getting bank loans and investing in real estate, and by when. At one point, I had purchased properties totaling $800,000, which meant I was only $200,000 short of my goal. And if it weren't for my networking group, I might have reasoned that this figure was close enough, and simply stopped. But the thought of telling them that I'd decided *not* to reach my goal was enough to get me through that final push.

In the end, my investments weighed in at $1.2 million, and that figure became the springboard for my next round of investing, because once you achieve a certain level of success, it's much easier to reach for the next level. But without that initial accomplishment, it is far harder—if not impossible—to imagine doing whatever it is you want to do.

How a Networking Group Zooms You Toward Your Goal

As we've just seen, a networking group can offer an enormous source of support when you're transforming your life—traveling from where you are to where you want to be, in the shortest time frame. A supportive group of business-oriented people can encourage you at every juncture, while offering their collective wisdom—their expertise and experience—to help you reach whatever you envision for yourself.

For example, when several of our members were determined to lose quite a lot of weight, the fitness professionals among us were able to offer valuable advice on the types of workouts they should begin to do, followed by more strenuous exercises when they began to see progress.

When I was gearing up to "dial for dollars" by asking local banks for investment loans, the bankers and finance professionals in our group were able to tell me how best to approach lending officers and what type of collateral I would need in order to convince them I was loan-worthy.

In a more generalized sense, the other positive aspect of being a member of a networking group is that we all model success for one another: Each time one of us succeeds in reaching one of our goals, that encourages and inspires everyone else. It's as if we create a collective energy of success that acts as a kind of "rocket fuel" that ensures the success of all our endeavors.

At the same time, I do want to mention that it's important to make sure that all the members of your group exhibit the qualities most conducive to succeeding; among these are being energetic, engaged, persistent, and able to believe that the realization of realistic but challenging goals is imminently possible.

If you are interested in exploring how a networking group can help you achieve your entrepreneurial goals, feel that you have the aforementioned qualities, and would like to be helped while helping others in turn, check out the online networking group available here: mitchdurfee.com/wolf-pack

In the next chapter, we'll take a longer look at the roles that beliefs and attitudes play in achieving your goals.

CHAPTER 7

STEP 4

HAVE A POSITIVE MENTAL ATTITUDE

HERE'S A SIMPLE WAY TO LINK STEP 3 (BUILD YOUR Network) and Step 4 (Have a Positive Mental Attitude) in the *Serve 2 Win* eight-step system, by making these two steps into a business mantra you can remember more easily:

If joining a networking group is a good way to get *external* support and encouragement . . . cultivating a positive mental attitude is a good way to get *internal* encouragement and support.

Your ultimate goal will manifest more quickly when you have both external and internal support coming to you on a consistent basis.

What *Is* a Positive Mental Attitude?

Despite how it may sound, Positive Mental Attitude (PMA) is a real term with its own Wikipedia page, and as the online encyclopedia notes, the concept was first publicly promoted by Napoleon Hill in 1937 during the Great Depression, when he published his classic self-help book *Think and Grow Rich*.

In Hill's first book, which continues to sell millions of copies eighty years later, he talked about the role that thoughts play in achieving wealth (or anything else you might want). More specifically, Hill advocated for thoughts that boost self-confidence, believing that anyone could achieve whatever they might desire, provided their thoughts were strongly and consistently positive and uplifting.

In the years since, Hill's concept of thinking your way to riches (or whatever you desire) has made its way into the realm of Positive Psychology—a branch of the larger field of psychology. And the term currently refers to having an optimistic and hopeful outlook, even while faced with life's many challenges, since those who practice PMA habitually seek ways around problems, rather than succumbing to negativity, self-doubt, and despair.

At the same time, Hill advocated for bolstering your Positive Mental Attitude by visualizing your goal as fully realized, while affirming it with phrases (affirmations) that reinforce that attainment. For instance, I might visualize the properties I want to acquire while repeating the affirmation "I now own all the properties I need for a passive income stream of six figures."

For those not familiar with affirmations, it may seem odd to say you have something when you obviously don't, but the reason for phrasing your manifestation goal this way comes from how our subconscious minds work. They do not know the difference between what is real and what is hoped for or imagined. Actually owning a bunch of properties, or saying that you own them when you don't yet, will register with your subconscious mind as equally true and real.

Meanwhile, manifestation works best when we broadcast the feeling we want to have—that happiness and fulfillment we'll feel, once we get what we want—*before* we actually get it. This is why affirmations that broadcast the feeling of already having what we desire are the fastest way to attract whatever we want.

That said, having a Positive Mental Attitude should not be confused with "wishful thinking" or thoughts we might consider PMA's ineffective cousin—as even if you maintain a Positive Mental Attitude on most days, you will still need to take action toward your goals (as I'll discuss in Chapter Eight).

What a PMA does is surround you with the kind of mental energy that's most conducive to attaining your goal.

Of course, negative thoughts do just the opposite, and you want to spend as little time as possible sending negative thoughts out into the world.

Another element of establishing and maintaining a Positive Mental Attitude that Hill discussed is the role of "vibrations," meaning the energy that creates, surrounds, and permeates everything that exists. Hill also believed in the importance of the subconscious mind in determining what shows up in our lives. But both of these elements of manifestation—our subconscious mind and our level of vibrational energy—are not visible to us, and therefore seem to be something we can't influence.

As it turns out, though, and as Hill points out in *Think and Grow Rich*, our thoughts and baseline attitude toward life's events—which are elements we *can* influence—will ultimately alter both our subconscious thoughts and the energetic vibrations emanating from us (which also form the energetic environment in which we habitually reside).

That being the case—the fact that it's in our best interest to create and maintain a positive mental attitude—the next question is, how can we consistently do that?

Got PMA?

You've probably noticed the same phenomenon that I have—and not just once or twice, but over and over again, because we often forget this particular cause-and-effect scenario. I understand that my thoughts influence my ability to reach my goals; what I often forget is that my thoughts influence my energy level, as well. For instance, when I'm giving myself the nutritious "food" of positive, uplifting, you-got-this thoughts, I feel empowered. I can handle anything that comes up. I have a strong belief that I'll succeed, because my energy is flowing freely.

But when I'm stuffing down the "junk food" of negative, doom-and-gloom thoughts, I can feel my energy flatten like a punctured tire. I feel weak and tired, and it seems like too much trouble to do anything at all, because my imminent failure feels inevitable.

And yet, since I'm responsible for the well-being of three businesses, giving in to negativity is simply not an option. I can't let myself feel disempowered, uninspired, and de-motivated for more than a few minutes. So when I feel down, I know it's time to check my mental soundtrack—the voice in my mind that's either broadcasting energy-lifting, high-five thoughts or broadcasting energy-draining, thumbs-down thoughts.

Invariably, what I'm telling myself (sometimes so faintly in the background that it's difficult to discern), as well as picturing, is a series of worst-case scenarios in my businesses that will most likely never happen. What *has* happened is that I've let myself feel a vague fear long enough for it to establish itself in the form of negative thoughts.

Fortunately, the way out is simple, quick, and easy. All I have to do is switch my thoughts from negative to positive, as easily as if I were switching one of those on-off toggle switches on my smart phone.

PMA & Vermont Winters

Perhaps you're thinking that all this positive mental attitude stuff sounds good, but wondering whether it works in actual practice—not to mention, whether it will work for *you*. So here's a real-life example of how my ability to switch off negative thoughts and turn on positive ones (something I've spent a lot of time practicing) helped my Grunts Move Junk business survive and thrive during a series of bone-chilling and snow-laden Vermont winters.

To set the scene for you, it's important to understand that every new business goes through what might be called a winter period. This occurs after that point where things had been percolating along nicely, building steadily, and your enthusiasm was strong and unwavering. And then, everything stops growing—much as it does in winter. At first, you wonder what you're doing wrong. After that, you begin to wonder if it's time to give up. Perhaps this really *isn't* the right place, you think, for this kind of business.

At this juncture, when throwing in the towel seems like a real possibility, you have to remind yourself of your larger service goal—your passion to make a meaningful contribution, one that meets real needs in the lives of all your customers and your employees. If that larger purpose is lacking, it can seem too hard to continue, once you hit the winter hibernation period.

But if you *do* have a strong commitment to serving others as your ultimate goal, you'll still need to support yourself during those times in the life of your business when things come to a standstill (as they do in nature during the cold months). But just like the natural cycle of the seasons, this pause time is a necessary period when your business is preparing for its next leap forward, for its upcoming burst of renewed life in the spring.

So here's how this kind of scenario played out in my first business. When actual winter arrived, after months of good, steady growth during which I'd been able to hire nearly thirty people, I was faced with the fact that it's hard to work outside in the cold, and it might be best to close for the season. And yet, I didn't want to do that; I felt responsible for all my employees. So I decided to get into the snow removal business. But there were some people who didn't want to work in the cold, our vehicles and snow equipment kept breaking down, we had a bunch of time-consuming flat tires, and record snowfall meant we were inundated with more customers than we could handle—all of them needing their driveways cleared at precisely the same time, so they could get to work. Meanwhile, I was personally working sixteen-hour days, seven days a week, just to keep everything running.

It was a good thing I had that larger purpose to aim for—my desire to help as many returning vets and first responders re-acclimate to civilian life as I could—or I might have spent more unproductive time feeling avalanched by winter problems.

As it was, I found a way to swim up to the surface for air by turning my attention to the many elements of my business that were doing well, and stacking them up like a success wall (that blocked out the current difficulties). These elements included the fact that we had a great referral rate, with a third of our customers actively referring new business to us; the fact that the phones were ringing nonstop; that we had a client base of 150 accounts; that we were handling fifteen customers a day with five teams; that new jobs were coming in fast and furious; and that we were giving back to the community in an important, visible way.

By using PMA-stacking, I successfully got myself out of a temporary funk and back into the business of providing service to those who needed it, while keeping all my employees on the payroll during the cold months. I have to say, having a Positive Mental Attitude really saved the day for me, just then.

But on most days, my PMA just helps me do what I do with more vim and vigor and unstoppable enthusiasm. That's no small thing, because it rubs off on all my employees and helps create a positive atmosphere within the company in general.

So hats off to Napoleon Hill for first realizing the importance of attitude in attracting into your life whatever you truly want in life.

CHAPTER 8

STEP 5

TAKE ACTION

NOTHING HAPPENS UNLESS YOU TAKE ACTION.

It's not enough to have the right values—the overall aim of serving others.

Nor is it enough to have clear goals that you've researched and studied, and want very much to attain.

It also isn't enough to have a supportive and inspiring networking group.

And even maintaining a Positive Mental Attitude is not, all by itself, enough.

That's because, without taking concrete steps toward your goal, you will always remain exactly where you are now.

And yet, since there is risk involved in taking action, you could be blindsided into thinking that, if you ace the four steps above, you will magically reach your goal. The mind is a wondrously complex aspect of our being, and it wants to protect us from harm—which it will do using any, and every, means. As a result, if the thought of taking a first step elicits fear, your mind may persuade you that you needn't take that step. Really, it says quietly, it's not necessary.

But here is how you can outsmart your self-protective mind: Just take any relatively easy step toward your goal, aiming to build up some momentum. Once you have a rolling start, taking steps will no longer be something your mind wants to help you escape. Do remember, though, to take those steps with the aforementioned four legs of support: your service values, your well-researched ultimate goal, the motivational cheerleading and information-sharing of your networking group, and your Positive Mental Attitude, maintained daily.

How I Took Real Steps to Reach My Goal

There is another step I recommend to my coaching clients, one I've only referenced indirectly above, and that is, before taking action, you need to acquire as much knowledge about your ultimate goal as possible, so your actions will be both appropriate and effective.

In my case, that meant committing to reading one book per week about launching a business, or about empowerment and motivation, or on real estate investing (I also learned to speed read, a valuable skill I recommend to all my coaching clients; information is available here: MitchDurfee.com/speed-read).

At the same time, I looked for successful people to model myself on, and I studied their strategies through audio books, podcasts, and YouTube videos.

Finally, I participated in group coaching—in which each member of the group shared information and wisdom from their area of expertise—through my networking group. (Just as an aside, it has made sense to me to more recently hire a personal coach and a business coach. Both have helped me grow quickly as a businessperson while accelerating my earnings.)

Once I'd acquired enough knowledge to discern which properties were good investments, an odd thing happened: I started seeing real estate opportunities everywhere. Driving along streets I'd driven down a zillion times, I suddenly saw rental property buildings selling for less than their market value—in other words, just what I was looking for.

Later on, I learned that this phenomenon is similar to what happens when you buy a new car. All at once, you're seeing cars just like yours everywhere you go. Whereas, before you got your new car, you never saw even one. This is due to our reticular activating system (RAS), which is the neurological term for our mind's ability to focus our attention on whatever is most meaningful to us—in other words, to prioritize a vast amount of constant sensory input. And, given the knowledge I acquired through reading and listening to audio books, I was newly aware of what a good rental property investment was, and began seeing them everywhere.

After that, taking action followed naturally, because once you have the background information you need, and your goals, vision, and direction are clear, it's game time. The only thing that will hold you back now is your fear.

What's the Fear About?

For those who have a long-term goal of launching their own small business, fear typically only figures into the equation when you are about to take action at the beginning, before you've fully committed to plunging into the fast-flowing stream of entrepreneurship.

Those first few steps into unknown territory are naturally more than a little frightening. On the other hand, fear also involves an element of excitement. More often than not, the thought of finally moving ahead with your goal is both frightening *and* exciting. Even so, the unknown soon becomes the known, and then the familiar, which is when fear dissolves of its own accord.

How to Get Past Those First Steps

Napoleon Hill (who spent two decades learning the techniques of 500 financially successful men in an era when a majority struggled economically during the Great Depression), realized that our thoughts give rise to those fears that hold us back from taking action. Hill realized, as well, that if we move our thoughts onto a positive thought loop, and away from a negative one, we can release the locking mechanism that our fear constitutes, and step into action without resistance.

Here's how I've experienced Hill's recommendation in the context of launching my own businesses. What I know, and what I remind myself of whenever I feel anxiety getting the upper hand, is that my mind controls my body, not vice versa. And so all I need to do is list the steps I need to take, and do the first one.

At the same time, I don't expect myself to get it 100 percent right on the first try. What I *do* expect to do, though, is set off toward my goal in the right direction, while making adjustments along the way.

Really, I can't emphasize enough the importance of taking steps toward your goal, of taking actions that will teach you more about how to get where you want to go than all the planning in the world ever will.

When you cast fear aside and get started, you are putting yourself on a path of learning how to get where you want to go. And like any journey, when you've completed it once, the next time is always several magnitudes easier.

That is not to say that it won't sometimes be hard or even painful in the beginning. You'll need to tolerate trying and failing at first—most of us do, often multiple times—but failing while trying isn't really failing. It's an experience of working with the realities of your chosen area of entrepreneurship, realities that will teach you how to succeed.

It is far more painful to never try at all because of vague fears. The people who are rewarded in this world are the ones who take action, and who, once they have a goal they've studied thoroughly and are committed to, go after it wholeheartedly.

You might even say that the one difference between people who achieve great things and those who leave this life with their ideas untested and unrealized, is the difference between those who are willing to take that first, awkward step, and those who allow their fears to prevent even a first step, so that their fear ultimately drowns out all their potential.

We only have so many days in this lifetime. Taking action enables us to make the most of each one.

CHAPTER 9

STEP 6

PROTECT YOUR TIME

TIME IS COMPLETELY EGALITARIAN. WE ALL HAVE the same number of hours each day. As a result, we could mistakenly assume that time has no particular value. After all, there are lots of undifferentiated potential work hours (forty to sixty hours, and sometimes more) in any given week, all of which add up to hundreds of barely noticed minutes.

But if we *were* to assume that, we would be wrong: time is actually a very limited resource.

We can't buy more of it.

We can't barter for a few extra hours.

And once any given period of time is gone, it's gone forever.

Time is irreplaceable. It's an "unrenewable" resource.

And yet, any goal we set for ourselves must be accomplished within the hours we have available—carved from the time we must devote to all our other responsibilities.

Protecting our time, if we want to succeed in creating an entrepreneurial enterprise, is a critically important strategy. It is also a skill, one we can learn to employ through trial and error, and a bit of practice, too.

Let's take a look at several ways we can cultivate the skill of protecting this most valuable resource: our time.

Pareto's Principle: How "Must-Do" Tasks Get Done

Vilfredo Pareto was a twentieth-century Italian economist who observed that a mere 20 percent of his country's population owned or controlled 80 percent of its wealth. Nearly four decades later, an American management expert named Dr. Joseph M. Juran applied Pareto's findings to the workplace, noting that 20 percent of any given workforce is generally responsible for 80 percent of the total results. As Dr. Juran subsequently concluded, that workforce could be separated into two groups: what he called "the vital few" and "the trivial many." By this he meant that a small percentage of workers were vital to the success of a business, while the majority were not vital at all.

We'll look at this idea again in a few minutes, but right now, I'd like to apply Pareto's 80/20 rule to something I first mentioned in Chapter Three. And that is, in order to make use of this rule as it applies to a day's workload (how 20 percent of your tasks will yield 80 percent of your results), it's wise to first divide your big list of tasks into four smaller categories:

- Do Now
- Delay Now
- Delegate Now
- Discard Now

While these categories are self-explanatory, the concept of dividing your tasks into buckets you can cope with more easily is itself a strategy that will solve such basic work problems as procrastination due to overwhelm. *And* its attendant problem: an inability to find a path through piles of tasks that seem equally important.

Just by discarding and delegating, you'll find that you have taken care of a large number of tasks that may have been weighing on you more heavily by the day. That bit of relief can free you enough to restore your energy and get you moving again, if you've been stuck in something resembling a "slough of despond" in your business. If, on the other hand, that is not the case, delegating and discarding will give you enhanced momentum—which is priceless during any workday.

As for the Do Now and Delay Now task buckets, once you have a clear idea of what to do and what to delay (and do remember to schedule your Delay Now tasks for a specific time in the future, so they will get done), you are ready to get to work on the last step in this process. And that is, dividing your Do Now tasks into two further buckets, Must Do and Should Do.

Here's how I handle my Do Now tasks, after I've divided them into Must Do and Should Do: I plan my time so that I address my Must Do tasks in the first two hours of the day. And, once those tasks are completed, I use the remaining six hours or so to address my Should Do tasks. The reason this is a good use of my time is probably clear, but I'll add that nothing feels better than completing tasks that will move my business forward.

In the end, the payoff of using divide-and-conquer strategies is really two-fold: You benefit your business *and* you improve your confidence in both your business and yourself. I'm so enthusiastic about this strategy that I'd like to underscore its benefits once more: completing your Must Do tasks first thing in your workday is just about guaranteed to boost your spirits, even on days when things seem to be moving in less-than-optimal directions in other areas.

The 80/20 Rule &
Your Employees

Now that we've applied Pareto's Principle to your workday tasks, I'd like to apply it to your workforce, as well. You'll recall that, at the beginning of this chapter, I mentioned Dr. Juran's application of Pareto's 80/20 rule to the American workplace. He discovered that the average business achieved its results because of the contributions consistently made by a mere 20 percent of its employees, while the remaining 80 percent did not contribute nearly as much.

In looking at my own businesses, I've found this to be true, as well, with one additional caveat: Not only do a smaller number of employees exemplify the kind of work ethic that every business owner wants to see, but if I cannot cut back on those employees who rely on my core group of workers to coast through their workday, I will soon have fewer "twenty percenters" pulling more than their fair share. In other words, the hard workers will get tired of being exploited by those who don't exhibit a conscientious approach to their jobs.

And so, apart from taking steps to upgrade my workforce—by letting go of those who aren't compatible with my goals—I also encourage greater productivity by using Parkinson's Law whenever appropriate.

Parkinson's Law:
Using the Expansion Theory of Work

In case you've not yet heard about this very useful insight, here's a bit of background:

During the mid-1950s, the British author, professor of naval history, and management expert Cyril Nothcote Parkinson wrote a book titled *Parkinson's Law.* In it, Professor Parkinson identified the chief reason bureaucracies are so often ineffective, and this reason he encapsulated in a succinct "law," which stated: "Work expands to fill the time available for its completion."

What Parkinson meant is that if you have a month to complete a task, you will probably find ways to not only procrastinate, but to make that task more complicated than it really needs to be, in order to fill up that four-week time frame. If, however, you only have two hours to get it done, you will probably complete that same task with half an hour to spare.

Human nature is such that many of us respond most strongly to urgency. But when there is no need for immediate action, many of us will put off doing a task until we *do* feel a sense of urgency—in which case, we'll apply ourselves and get the job done. Perhaps not well. And perhaps just in the nick of time, but at least, it will be done.

As a result, I've learned to make use of the Parkinson's Law tendencies we all share when managing each group of my workforce. For instance, if there are 62 business inquiry emails that need to be read and answered or deleted, by the end of the workday at 4:00 PM, I tell my three-person office staff that, if they finish all those emails by 3:00 PM, they can then go home.

Of course, I've already calculated that dealing with an average email will take them between three and seven minutes, so they should be able to get through twenty or more per hour. In other words, I make sure that what I'm proposing is realistic and fair. However, the incentivizing "carrot" of getting to leave an hour early does work wonders for their motivation—in combination with a "shrink-wrap" time frame—every time.

It works wonders for me, too: I reward myself for completing my Must Do and Should Do tasks by scheduling nearly 25 percent of my time, each month, to read books, listen to podcasts, and attend conferences by nationally known coaches and business experts. I do this because when I got back from serving twenty-seven months in Iraq and Afghanistan, I felt as though I was behind by the same number of months. All my friends had opted to go to college, while I entered the military, thinking it would become my career. When that didn't work out as planned and I came back to Vermont, I felt as if I'd left the gate late and was at a distinct disadvantage to all my peers.

To make up for that "deficit," I now devote approximately one-fourth of my time to absorbing strategies, tools, expertise, and wisdom from people who have become my teachers and models for entrepreneurship—and for life.

You could say this is what inspired me to develop what I call "Durfee's Dictim," which encourages fledgling entrepreneurs to learn all they can, before executing as well as they can, and then repeating this two-part process over again, while expecting to excel.

The catchier version goes like this: Learn, Execute, Repeat > Excel

As entrepreneurs, we never stop learning. That's what makes business ownership challenging and exciting, so it becomes a grand adventure—one that's self-guided and self-initiated.

CHAPTER 10

STEP 7

BUILD YOUR TEAM

WHEN I LAUNCHED MY FIRST COMPANY, GRUNTS Move Junk, I found myself in the same position nearly everyone finds themselves in when starting a small business: I did every job in my company. In other words, I wore all the hats: CEO, Vice President, COO, Marketing Director, Phone Answerer / Jobs Receiver, and Worker (providing the moving services my business offered). There wasn't any other choice at that stage. If I didn't do it, it didn't get done.

This was true even though I almost immediately hired a small staff of military veterans to help me do the actual "grunt" work, the physical labor. And it was true even though I certainly wasn't playing to my strengths by taking care of all the paperwork that running a small business inevitably entails.

Outsourced Work & In-House Staff

But we survived. And my business entered the next phase of its development, allowing me to hire a phone-answering service to take calls during business hours and relay messages when I called in. This outsourced job alone doubled our income and more than paid for itself. The only problem was, customer satisfaction went south, because while customer requests were noted, new clients had to wait for me to call them back with more detailed information, and that sometimes took an entire day.

Half a year later, I was able to hire a receptionist / phone answerer who worked out of our Grunts office. This was a big improvement, more than tripling our customer satisfaction, as our potential and existing clients could talk to a knowledgeable person during their first call, rather than a third-party message-taker.

After another year and a half, I was ready to make a bigger leap forward in my business, one I'd wanted to do almost from the beginning, but didn't yet have the profit margin to accommodate. I hired a Chief Operating Officer, a man I was sure would fill this position well—because I used the method outlined in *Who*, the Geoff Smart and Randy Street how-to-hire-the-right-people book. Smart and

Street propose a commonsense, yet not widely practiced approach to finding and hiring what they call "A players," people whose skills are a perfect fit with their job. The *Who* authors advocate a preliminary two-step process that begins with understanding your company's culture (win at all costs, for example, or ethics-driven), and after that is clear, their process turns to understanding the outcomes you want your new hire to achieve (organize your workforce more efficiently, for example, or achieve record sales).

This saves a lot of time that would otherwise be wasted with typical recruitment interview mistakes, such as thinking trick questions (how would you handle a difficult boss?) will unearth the "real" interviewee beneath the false front a stressful job interview can elicit or using inane interview questions (what do you like to do in your spare time?) in the vain attempt to discover whether this candidate is stable and well-rounded, or even reverting to that favorite fallback position of going with your gut feeling about the interviewee (I know he's a good guy because I "read" people well).

Instead of using these ineffective interviewing techniques, the "street-smart" method recommends matching the skills and personality of the person you are considering with your company's culture, as well as the skills required to achieve the outcomes you want. Seems fairly obvious, doesn't it? Alas, it's not obvious to many HR people and their companies. As a small business owner, though, you can't afford to make costly hiring mistakes.

To avoid a mistake when I hired a COO for my Vermont office, I used the *Who* approach and onboarded an executive who was a top "A" player. I knew he would get things done (with no supervision on my part) and would take ownership of his job and my company's goals, helping me achieve milestones and grow the business.

What did I look for when I hired him? Our company culture is, first of all, about the service we offer; we exist to serve the communities we work in (while serving our employees at the same time), and we care about building our reputation as a group and as individual workers who go above and beyond to help our customers. I needed someone who could buy into that service ethic, who believed in what we were doing. Jeff Goode (I'll use a pseudonym to ensure his privacy) did buy in to both, and so earned a big check mark on my list of desired attributes.

Second, I needed someone with the ability to see the big picture (my company's potential); to understand its present rate of growth; and to handle its large and small managerial tasks on a day-to-day, week-to-week, and month-to-month basis. In short, I needed someone who cared enough about my business to take over many of my management jobs with an ownership mind-set, as well as someone who had the organizational and people skills to do that with ease. Jeff had the past experience, the demonstrated skills, and the qualities of character I was looking for, so he got another big check mark there.

And what did I gain by investing in a COO?

I knew it was time for me to focus on the long view in this business, so what I gained was the time and added energy to do that. Jeff allowed me to turn my attention to more expansive marketing efforts (partnering with other local businesses, for instance, to offer package deals). And I was also able to focus more of my time on moving the Grunts Move Junk business model into parts of the country we hadn't yet looked into.

The CEO's SWOT

There's another aspect of the team-building process that's nearly as important as hiring the right person for the right job. And that is, the process of evaluating your own skills as business owner—so you can delegate those jobs that are not the strongest parts of your skill set. The reason this is critical to your team-building effort is the overwhelming tendency for those who have an entrepreneurial personality to believe that no one else can do anything as well as they can. There's a danger, as a result, of getting trapped "in the weeds," and handling all the minutiae rather than focusing on the larger needs of the business. To rescue entrepreneurs from this tendency, the SWOT (Strengths, Weaknesses, Opportunities, and Threats) self-evaluation tool is extremely useful.

In fact, when I looked at my own SWOT, trying to objectively evaluate each of the four elements, I was able to see more clearly where my Strengths actually were (larger vision, marketing, team inspiration), and where my Weaknesses resided (paperwork, managing people day-to-day, irritability when extremely tired). The point wasn't to beat myself up, but to realize that I needed to hire people who could compensate for those areas in which I wasn't as strong, and to arrange my organization so I could make better use of my inherent Strengths. As soon as that was economically feasible, this is exactly what I did.

As for my Opportunities, I had all along planned to expand Grunts Move Junk—as a business model beneficial to returning vets and their communities, in many locations nationally. At the same time, I built up other Opportunities (especially in the area of real estate investing) so I could achieve my ultimate goal, which was to live on passive income and help others as a business coach and angel investor, while living at the beach and scuba diving every day. So it seemed as if I'd worked on my Opportunities pretty well, at least for this stage of my entrepreneurial development. At the same time, I had also increased the scope of my Opportunities by spending a lot of time at empowerment and business-building conferences, seminars, and workshops, learning all that I could from people who had succeeded in doing what I wanted to do.

Finally, my Threats area looked remarkably "unpopulated," because I'd invested in multiple business areas and hadn't relied on any one effort or initiative to carry the full weight of my long-term goals.

That said, though, I did recognize that my Grunts business had a "low barrier to entry," which meant just about anyone could copy our business model and pose a threat to us through competition. As a result, we consistently evaluated our level of professionalism and sought to provide more value to our customers, as a way of setting us apart from any other businesses that might try to enter our territory.

SWOT & Your Business

The SWOT evaluation tool can be very useful for gaining clarity about where your business currently stands, relative to its company Strengths, Weaknesses, Opportunities, and Threats. And when I sat down to run Grunts through this four-part tool using a series of checklists, I immediately saw that, while we were well-positioned locally to expand our client base and recruit new staff to handle the added workload, we were ultimately going to be limited by our small-town location. As a result, I took steps to move the business beyond my hometown, bringing it to neighboring towns, in order to take advantage of a nearly inexhaustible need for snowplowing during our Vermont winters, along with a need for moving services during the rest of the year. What I actually did was take our one Weakness (which could be seen as a Threat, as well)—our locale—and turn it around, making it into an Opportunity.

You can use a similar strategy with your business, by identifying a potential or future Weakness or Threat and flipping it into an Opportunity. This is fairly easy to do, since most Threats contain an Opportunity you may take advantage of by playing to your company's Strengths.

The A, B, & C of Team Building

I mentioned the hazards of hiring people who are "B" and "C" players—as opposed to more-desirable "A" players— in Chapter Three, but I'd like to revisit this concept now, in order to underscore the reasons why you would be wise to avoid hiring people whose skills don't match those needed for the outcomes you seek.

To begin, it's important to emphasize that *your* "B" and "C" players might be another company's "A" players. In other words, it's not that they lack skills, but they lack the skills needed to succeed at the job for which you're interviewing them. And that means it's not up to *them* to measure up to your needs; it's up to *you* to know what needs you have—in other words, which skills your job requires.

For instance, I may have the drive and the vision to create a series of companies while investing in real estate, but I would not be an "A" player hire for a position that was primarily paperwork. So the solution, again, is what the authors of *Who* suggest, which is to understand the outcomes you seek, and then locate people with the skills to create those results.

In the next chapter, we'll look at step eight in the *Serve 2 Win* process, and discuss effective ways of positioning yourself for success as a small business owner.

CHAPTER 11

STEP 8

POSITION YOURSELF TO WIN

WHILE THE APPROACH I'M SUGGESTING IN *SERVE 2 Win* is all about positioning yourself to win as a self-employed entrepreneur (and the steps outlined in previous chapters will help you get there), it's important to know what it looks like to put yourself in a winning position. And one of the easiest ways to see something more clearly is to take a look at everything that it *isn't*.

So here are some wrong turns I've made myself and have seen others make—both those I've known peripherally, and those I've met at business and motivational workshops.

Thinking You Already Know Everything

Ironically, deciding to become an entrepreneur means starting your career or work life from scratch. You may already be a success in some other field or endeavor, but when you start your own business, you are inevitably the new kid on the block. Your new business has to make friends, forge alliances, and generally find a way to fit in. And you yourself have to learn all the ins and outs of running your particular kind of business. That will take a bit of time, because there's a lot to learn. Much of it will come from attempts that aren't what you hoped—in other words, you'll do your fair share of falling down and getting back up again.

For some people, all of this is fine and good, and no big deal. They're perfectly happy embracing the beginner's role of someone eager to soak up all the information and experience they possibly can. They enjoy the process of learning; it's an adventure to them.

For others, there is nothing so excruciating as being someone who is not already an expert, someone who knows relatively little about whatever they are trying to accomplish. When people feel that way, they might revert to one of two fallback postures: 1) Pretending to know more than they do, while deciding that others have nothing to teach them that they don't already know; 2) Hiring people to take over much of the "heavy lifting" in setting up their business, before they understand enough about their business and its needs to do so knowledgeably.

Both of these fallback postures will ultimately fail because these entrepreneurs are failing to invest themselves in their business. The first type wants to avoid the effort of learning, and the second wants to avoid the effort of working to set up a new business.

But if one thing characterizes entrepreneurial endeavors and the people who take them on, it's the need and the willingness to work overtime—over time—as that's the level of commitment needed to achieve this goal.

Being Too Easily Discouraged by Early Stumbles

You may remember learning to ride a bicycle as a child, and how that process was anything but exhilarating. You'd wobble along unsteadily for a few feet, then start to fall over, before being saved by the strong arm of a parent. To you, at that stage, all those older kids who rode their bikes as easily as they walked seemed like child-gods, kids who were blessed with special powers.

Weeks later, your body seemed to have an aha moment. All of a sudden, you were riding up and down the driveway with perfect balance. After that, you promptly forgot what it was like to learn how to ride a bike because, once you learned, your body never forgot. It just became another part of your physical skill set.

Launching a new business is kind of like learning to ride a bicycle. There will be wobbling. There will be frustration. It will seem as if others understand something that is beyond your ability to grasp. So there will be the temptation, again and again, to throw in the towel and give up. But that makes no more sense than it does for a child to give up when learning how to ride a bicycle.

If you persist, if you pick yourself up after every spill, you will eventually learn what you need to learn. After that, you'll continue to learn as you enter every new stage of your business's growth and evolution.

But if you don't persist, then it could be that your goal doesn't match your true interests and desires. In which case, it may be best to find another one. And that would mean your inability to persist may have been telling you something.

If you don't persist for some other reason—a tendency to get discouraged too easily, say—then it might be a good idea to build up your "persistence muscles" before attempting something that requires a particularly strong ability to persist, over time. Start small, get stronger one step at a time, then come back to your original goal and try again.

Wanting It to Be Easier Than It Is

It's always a good idea to practice PMA (Positive Mental Attitude) whenever you try something new, strenuous, and complex. Believing in yourself, thinking you can do something, goes a long way towards helping you actually do it.

However—just as thinking you already know everything, or getting discouraged too easily, can sabotage your efforts to launch an entrepreneurial business—wanting your launch to be easier than it really is can leave you feeling as though you've failed, when all you've actually done is encounter reality.

You could say that becoming an entrepreneur means believing you can, and holding on to your belief, even as you come face-to-face with the normal ups and downs of creating a new enterprise from scratch.

Sometimes, that's harder than other times, of course, which brings us full circle to our original point: what positioning yourself to win looks like in actual practice. And, as you might expect, what it looks like is the ability to exhibit positive qualities and characteristics—which are the exact opposite of the negative traits described above.

Being Willing to Learn

No one is born with the knowledge, skills, and experience to create a successful business. Entrepreneurs learn how to do what they need to do by studying the experience of others who have succeeded at something similar to what they aspire to do. After that, brand new entrepreneurs become increasingly skilled at adapting what successful other people can teach them, and using it for their specific situation. In other words, they are willing to learn from the mistakes and breakthroughs of those who have succeeded in accomplishing similar goals.

In my own case, as I mentioned earlier, while I entered the military instead of going to college, once I decided to leave my post-military, "hours for dollars" job as a mechanic rebuilding car engines, I created what I see now was my own Entrepreneurial College curriculum. Although, even when I was still in the service, I began listening to podcasts about real estate and business, and then, once I returned to the States, I went at it full throttle, attending workshops, seminars, and conferences.

In the end, I may not have walked away with a degree, but I did become the owner of three businesses—one of which is on its way to moving into a handful of locations, with plans for nationwide expansion, over time. And if you think about it, not many college graduates are equipped to earn a living once they leave the classroom. Whereas, my self-generated curriculum prepared me to one day be free of the day-to-day grind of the work world entirely, so I can enjoy serving others without competing demands on my time. In other words, once I'm totally self-sufficient and living on passive income, I'd like to help others find their best path to a similar kind of freedom, by showing them how I did what I did. (What you get from others, you can turn around and, down the road, give back to others, albeit a different group of others.)

Being Willing to Fall Down & Pick Yourself Up

There is really no such thing as winning the first time you try, at least not with something as complex as creating a business. Instead, you make a series of attempts, some of which will fail, and some of which will succeed. But you can learn from the failures (as well as the successes) and then leapfrog forward into your next series of attempts. Doing so is what I call "incremental growth," the step-by-step growth that occurs in the beginning of a new enterprise.

For instance, when I first started Grunts Move Junk, I didn't yet know how to hire people who were self-starting and would take ownership of their responsibilities, within the larger context of my business as a whole. Instead, I made hiring mistakes. I onboarded people who didn't want to be coached or trained for their job, which meant I had to work through their defensiveness. A simple fifteen-minute task would take an hour to explain, because these people wouldn't listen when I explained what needed to be done, and would be sullen when what they did had to be done over again. The one good thing about all this was that it led me to turn to experts. I read books about hiring techniques and learned the difference between "A" players and the "B" and "C" players who are more trouble than they are worth, especially in a small business in which everyone needs to pull their full weight.

But here's the happy ending to this story: Once I made it through the incremental or step-by-step phase of my business's development (in which I did have to repeatedly pick myself up after falling down), I began to experience geometric growth, or business growth that arrives in chunks rather than small steps.

After Grunts was in place and was humming along smoothly alongside my real estate selling and investing work, I was able to create offshoot businesses that served my customers within both businesses. One of these was a moving supplies business; another was a landscaping business. I launched these because, when people first move into a new house, they often want to re-landscape. As a result, I geometrically grew my business by first selling them the boxes and other supplies they needed to pack all their belongings; then I moved all their belongings; and finally, I helped them beautify their new home with custom landscaping.

Being Willing to Persist

For the most part, I've focused in previous chapters on the brighter side of entrepreneurship—how to succeed and how to maintain a positive mental attitude—that sort of thing. But now I'd like to be blunt, because I don't want you to think launching a business is—or should be—easy and fun, every single day. If you think that, you could easily believe there's something wrong if you have a not-so-good day or week.

So here's the truth: There are days when it seems my businesses are not worth the effort it takes to sustain them. On one of those days, for example, after I hired a marketing firm to redesign all our Grunts Move Junk ads, which pointed to landing pages on our website, I was completely stymied. The marketing firm had completed their work six weeks late and had screwed up our landing page links—even loading some with typos. Meanwhile, we'd blown our marketing budget and still didn't have a fully functional site. At this point, I considered shutting down the business, because growing it depended upon advertising, and our ad campaign seemed hopeless in the middle of that depressing moment.

But, as always when faced with an impasse in my business, I began to contemplate the alternative, which meant working for someone else (and building *their* success and dream life, rather than my own) and doing so for far less than I could make on my own, while having no job security, no financial security, and no way of exiting this hours-for-dollars treadmill in the future. So I backed away from the thought of giving up, gave myself ten minutes of PMA immersion, and got back at it.

In the instance above, my in-house team and I rebuilt our website, created new Facebook ads, tuned up our adwords with a click-to-call feature, as well as retargeting and posting YouTube videos—all of which we executed during an all-night workfest. In the end, that business-saving work of ours became the impetus and the basis for another business—my Online Start Up Box business, which helps entrepreneurs get their new businesses set up online.

In the next chapter, we'll take a look at some of the ways I can assist you in starting your own business, in a more direct way.

CHAPTER 12

A FEW CLOSING THOUGHTS
SHOULD WE KEEP TALKING?

IN THE PREVIOUS CHAPTER, I MENTIONED MY LONG-term goal of living on passive income and being free to help people launch one or more business enterprises—in other words, helping those who want to do what I've done (or am doing).

In the past few years, I've been moving ahead with this two-part goal by coaching more than five hundred fledgling entrepreneurs, while also getting closer to my passive income breakout point (though I'll need a few more years to finally get there).

But you may wonder why, when I could do anything at all—once I no longer have to work for living—I'd want to help fledgling entrepreneurs. And here's the answer: When

I was a returning veteran, I had a difficult time adjusting to civilian life; I had to learn, all over again, the ins and outs of thriving in civilian culture. Once I'd made that transition from military to civilian life, I then struggled with how to move forward with my career—how to get off the hours-for-dollars treadmill, and move beyond meeting basic expenses while carrying increasing amounts of debt. Eventually, as I mentioned in earlier chapters, I did figure things out—largely with the help of a handful of well-known business and motivational science experts.

At the same time, I found myself reaffirming something I'd experienced again and again, which is that nothing beats the good feeling of being able to help someone with the knowledge or skills I can offer them. So while it may seem altruistic to help others, it's also the best way to help myself—*and* others, at the same time.

Of course, there's more to it than that. The other part of pursuing this long-term goal comes from the fact that I know what it's like to be a military veteran, and I know many veterans who shared my feeling of being lost and rudderless after returning from combat. (We've all heard the dismal statistics about unemployed, homeless, and struggling vets who feel tossed aside when their military service is over.)

So one of my main aims is to help veterans and first responders transition back into civilian life in a number of ways, including through the Grunts Move Junk businesses in several states, and business coaching (see MitchDurfee. com and Serve2Win.com), another element of which is my business planning / marketing / branding agency (OnlineStartUpBox.com).

To give you an idea of how I coach new entrepreneurs through the process of launching their small businesses, I'd like to tell you a bit about my philosophy of coaching and then introduce you to a couple of my clients.

In a nutshell, my experience as a business coach (and as a coaching client myself) has taught me that the main benefit of coaching doesn't come from pushing someone out of a life rut and onto a more productive life path. That kind of heavy lifting can never be the coach's role.

When someone doesn't know where they want to go and what they want to achieve, a coach can't create that vision for them. And, to be candid, a coach really shouldn't take on that job. For no client will fully buy into a vision that he or she has not had a hand in creating. A coach who *does* insist on creating a new life vision for a client, will end up pulling and pushing him or her toward a goal the coach may want, but the client may not. And it's easy to see how well *that* will work out.

What a coach *can* do, though, is act as an experienced and knowledgeable guide, helping a client clarify the vision of where he wants to go, and why he wants to go there.

And, once a client has his vision in place, an experienced coach can assist his client in designing achievable goals that, one step at a time, will take him on the journey of realizing the larger vision.

Along the way, there may be times when a client reaches an impasse, or hits a wall in his growth and evolution. And then, an experienced coach can step in with insight and direction that help that client get back on track and moving forward again. (What I often tell my clients is that by walking where I have walked, I can help them avoid the hidden land mines in launching a business.)

In fact, my client Joe Garcia is a case in point. A veteran who returned home to Massachusetts, he reached out to me because, after reading books by top motivational gurus, as I had done, he was ready to take the next step. We discussed the idea he had for launching his own business, but nothing had really come together for him, just yet. Then, one day, he jokingly asked when I was going to bring Grunts Move Junk to his state. "When you're ready to launch that business," I answered. And we were off to the races, with Joe eager to open a Grunts business in his hometown.

I knew Joe would do really well, because he always exuded enthusiasm, energy, and a positive attitude—in addition to making sure he obtained the education he needed to get his new business off to a great start.

Another client, Zac Tucker, needed a different kind of help. Zac lives in Colorado and launched his moving company in an area where the competition was extremely fierce. So he was struggling to get a consistent stream of leads from higher-paying customers.

I helped him find new marketing opportunities while assisting him in designing his website, and then I showed him how to create systems to manage his funnel for new leads more efficiently, thus freeing his time for other pursuits—like managing the work his company was hired to do.

My client Chris Kelly had an entirely different kind of business in mind: He wanted to be a successful real estate investor, so he could move toward the freedom of a high-level stream of passive income. When I asked Chris for some feedback on our eighteen-month coaching relationship, here's what he wrote back: "Having you as a mentor and friend helped me understand that the potential to do great things was not out of my reach (Chris bought and sold nearly 1.5 million dollars' worth of real estate in the time we worked together). But," he added, "I never would have been able to do this by myself. The lengthy period needed to flip a property would have knocked me out of the real estate game before I even got started. So I owe you considerable thanks for streamlining the investing process for me, and helping me to attain my goals."

As I mentioned earlier, my role as a coach is largely about helping my clients avoid the various land mines that launching a business can present, and because I've walked through the small business launch terrain multiple times, I can easily warn them away from those pitfalls.

If you think coaching would be a good idea for you, and you'd like assistance in moving toward your personal vision and long-term goal, you can contact me at MitchDurfee.com (scroll to the bottom of my home page for the contact form).

As I say on my site, "I (heart) success."

Mitchdurfee.com

OnlineStartUpBox.com

GruntsMoveJunk.com

FreeVThomeValue.com

Serve2win.com

Mitch.Durfee@Gmail.com

CPSIA information can be obtained
at www.ICGtesting.com
Printed in the USA
BVHW011958241118
533897BV00004B/28/P